Inviting and Welcoming New People

Evangelism Study Series

Volume 2

Larry M. Dentler

faithQuest
the trade imprint of Brethren Press
Elgin, Illinois

Inviting and Welcoming New People
Evangelism Study Series, Volume 2
Larry M. Dentler

Copyright © 1992 by Brethren Press
faithQuest, the trade imprint of Brethren Press, 1451 Dundee Avenue, Elgin, Illinois 60120

Biblical quotations, unless otherwise noted, are from the New Revised Standard Version of the Bible, copyrighted 1989 by the Division of Christian Education, National Council of Churches, and are used by permission.

Cover design by Jeane Healy

96 95 94 93 92   5 4 3 2 1

Library of Congress Cataloging-in-Publication Data

Dentler, Larry M.
    Inviting and welcoming new people / Larry M. Dentler.
       p. cm.
    ISBN 0-87178-451-3
    1. Evangelistic work. I. Title.

BV3790.D476 1991
269'.2 2–dc20
                                     91-34232
                                         CIP

Manufactured in the United States of America

Contents

Purpose of the Study

1. To explore scriptures that provide insights and models for inviting and welcoming new people.
2. To discern learnings that call for personal action
3. To respond to those calls
4. To support others in their commitments to study and action

Introduction

"How could they have faith in one they had never heard of?" (Romans 10:14 NEB). Those words of the Apostle Paul sum up our reason for inviting and welcoming persons to faith. Our witness opens doors for individuals to discover the reality of Christ and Christ's community.

We are called to tell others about Jesus. Not with some magic formula for salvation. Not with some special combination of phrases said in just the right way. But through words and actions that are inviting.

Somewhere along the way we have lost our enthusiasm for guiding sisters and brothers into the family of faith. We have failed to embrace those outside of our fellowship.

In the following chapters we will rediscover the challenge to be inviters and welcomers. We will explore the wideness of that call. We will look at biblical models for sharing in this vital task.

These eight chapters expand on four keys for inviting and welcoming first introduced in chapter six ("Inviting and Welcoming New People") of the evangelism study booklet New Life for All. The keys are: (1) reaching one's existing network of relationships; (2) sensing receptive and right moments; (3) adopting a gracious, non-pushy style; (4) offering warm and open hospitality.

As you share in this study, may you experience anew the joy of inviting and welcoming others to faith. May God be present and guide you as you explore this vital part of Christian witness!

Suggestions for Participants and Leaders

For All Group Members

1. Pray daily for yourself and other group members to
   a. Become increasingly aware of God's presence and power;
   b. Discern God's messages presented in the scriptures;
   c. Recognize and use opportunities for communicating the gospel.

2. Prepare thoroughly for each session by
   a. Beginning well in advance;
   b. Using the PREPARATION FOR THE NEXT SESSION sections in the book as a guide;
   c. Reading the scripture text;
   d. Writing in the space provided your first responses to the passage;
   e. Reading the chapter;
   f. Using the REFLECTING ON THE SCRIPTURES questions to pause in your reading and allow yourself some time to meditate just on the scripture for five to ten minutes;
   g. Using RESPONDING TO THE SCRIPTURES to contemplate how the scripture touches your life and how you might change in light of your learnings;
   h. Marking phrases and writing questions and comments in the margin in order to remember and reinforce what you are learning.

3. Be a helpful group member by
    a. Attending all sessions;
    b. Practicing good listening skills;
    c. Enabling others to feel included, valued, and secure in sharing;
    d. Support other group members in their efforts to discern and respond to God's call for their lives.

4. If you are using a paraphrased or amplified version such as The Living Bible, be sure you also read the scripture texts in a standard translation such as the New Revised Standard Version or the New International Version.

5. Be aware that this study is typical of most areas of life. You will "reap what you sow." You will receive from it in proportion to what you give to it.

6. Be aware also that this study calls for action responses to learnings. In addition to studying this book and participating in discussion sessions, you will be applying what you learn to your daily life.

For Leaders

1. In preparation for your leadership role, complete the sentences in REFLECTING ON THE SCRIPTURES and RESPONDING TO THE SCRIPTURES found in each chapter. Mark the sentences in RESPONDING TO THE SCRIPTURES that you feel would be most helpful to the group.

2. Be prepared to share your thoughts and feelings as a way to encourage group involvement.

3. Begin and end sessions promptly.

4. During each session
    a. Begin with prayer for openness to the mind of Christ and the leading of the Spirit.
    b. Read the scripture text aloud.
    c. Discuss initial responses to the scripture.

    d. Discuss the sentences in REFLECTING ON THE SCRIPTURE.

    e. Discuss the sentences in RESPONDING TO THE SCRIPTURE.

    f. Invite additional comments.

    g. Review the PREPARATION FOR THE NEXT SESSION.

    h. Close with an appropriate song, prayer, or affirmation of faith.

5. Guide the discussions of RESPONDING TO THE SCRIPTURES toward specific, appropriate, individual responses so that time is not spent on generalities which lead to little or no action.

6. Monitor the time carefully to allow at least for discussion of all of the questions you decided would be most helpful.

7. Involve participants by inviting them ahead of time to lead in prayer, to dramatize the scripture, to prepare an appropriate closing, etc.

8. Allow for all points of view to be expressed by group members. It is not essential that everyone speak, but it is important that no one or two person(s) dominate the discussion and that everyone knows that they have the right to speak.

9. At the end of Session 4 ask participants to prepare for Session 5 by completing RESPONDING TO THE CALL FOR ACTION as well as the usual PREPARATION FOR THE NEXT SESSION.

10. Begin Session 5 with a brief sharing of what the participants have written in response to items one through four for RESPONDING TO THE CALL FOR ACTION. Divide into small groups of three or four persons each and allow about ten minutes for this sharing. Watch the time carefully.

11. Begin Sessions 6, 7, and 8 with a time of sharing as a total group or in twos or threes. Ask how participants are doing with their responses to calls for action. Encourage participants to support one another in their efforts. Allow about ten minutes for this and watch the time carefully.

12. Allow time at the end of Session 8 for the completing of and sharing of responses to RESPONDING TO THE CALL FOR ACTION.

13. Evaluate the past session prior to planning for the coming one.

1

Witnesses, With Power!

Purpose

- To celebrate Christ's call to be witnesses energized by the power of the Holy Spirit

Reading the Scriptures

Read and consider Acts 1:8.
My first responses to this passage are . . .

Exploring the Scriptures

The book of Acts is the exciting account of the life and ministry of the first Christians. The author of Acts is usually thought to be Luke the physician, the author of the Gospel of Luke. These "acts of the apostles" then are actually volume two in his account of "the things which have been accomplished among us" (Luke 1:1).

"Doctor Luke" begins the first chapter of Acts where he left off in his gospel–with the Great Commission. In essence he repeats the commission in Acts 1:8 as he calls those first Christians to receive power and bear witness to the ends of the earth.

The setting is the Mount of Olives. This well-known biblical site is located just to the east of Jerusalem. It consists of three hills rising up from the Kidron Valley. In the days of the early church it was thickly wooded with olive trees.

Lloyd J. Ogilvie comments that this particular time "when the apostles met together with Jesus" (Acts 1:6 TEV) seems to have been an in-between period after "the lightning of the incarnation" and "the thunder of Pentecost."[1]

As they stand on the Mount of Olives, Jesus prepares his disciples for his departure. He readies them to be the church, which in Acts is a dynamic, empowered church. The words of verses 2-4 (TEV) reflect this activity: "gave instructions" (v. 2); "showed himself," "talked with them about the Kingdom of God" (v. 3); "gave them this order . . . 'wait for the gift my Father promised'" (v. 4).

In Acts 1:3 we are told that this time of preparation lasted forty days. This is reminiscent of the forty days at the beginning of Christ's ministry (Luke 4:1-12), which was also a period of preparation. Perhaps he is seeking to end his mission the way it began.

Such a time of preparation, however, is not a dormant time. The words of Acts 1:6 (TEV) suggest that the disciples are full of excitement and anticipation. The reality of the risen Christ rekindles old dreams. "Lord, will you at this time give the Kingdom back to Israel," they blurt out like impatient children on Christmas morning.

What do they mean by that question? Like most Jews of their time they are convinced that as the chosen people of God they are destined to be at the center of an earthly, political kingdom established by God. After years of living under the rule of Assyrians, Babylonians, Persians, Greeks, or Romans, the thought of ruling with God is a liberating thought!

But Jesus indicates that they are not to concern themselves with a visible earthly kingdom—at least not yet. The times and occasions for such a political realm are uncertain and "not for you to know" (v. 7). However, there is much to do. The larger vision of the kingdom of God needs to be shared—a vision that is not dependent on a particular place and government, a vision that transcends politics, class, and region.

That's what I need witnesses for, Jesus says to those first apostles. I need ambassadors who will shout the news that I am Lord of all! "You will be filled with power when the Holy Spirit comes on you, and you *will be witnesses for me* in Jerusalem, in all of Judea and Samaria, and to the ends of the earth" (italics added) (v. 8 TEV).

A key ingredient in this larger sharing of the kingdom is the promise of power. In the original New Testament Greek, the word for power is dunamis. Literally, in this context, dunamis means a miraculous means of might, strength, or force.[2] Not surprisingly, our word dynamite is derived from this Greek root.

Acts has six other references to dunamis (3:12; 4:7, 33; 6:8; 8:10; and 10:38). Perhaps the most vivid is Acts 4:33 where Luke records that "With great power the apostles gave witness to the resurrection of the Lord Jesus, and God poured rich blessings on them all" (TEV).

We live in a "power-full" world. Our vocabulary and daily experiences overflow with images of power, wealth, and influence. The first apostles, however, are a "power-less" group, living in a world dominated by the iron-fisted ways of Rome. To be promised power is a great and exhilarating possibility.

But they are promised power for a purpose. They are empowered to be Christ's witnesses. The Greek word for witnesses is martures. Initially martures, from which we get our word "martyr," had a legal connotation. A witness, a marture, was "one who remembers and can tell about something."[3] Through the centuries, however, the meaning of martures expanded and deepened. Donald Carson traces its development:

    a. one who gives evidence, in or out of court
    b. one who gives solemn witness or affirmation (e.g., of one's faith)
    c. one who witnesses to personal faith, even in the threat of death
    d. one who witnesses to personal faith by the acceptance of death
    e. one who dies for a cause—a "martyr."[4]

In its most radical sense then, a witness not only remembers and testifies but is so concerned about truth that he or she is ready to give up his or her own life to defend it.

Reflecting on the Scriptures

1. What does the coming of the Holy spirit bring, as told in Acts 1:8?

2. What human action is called for in this verse?

3. What other scriptures (if any) does this passage bring to mind?

Applying the Scriptures

Power

Power like that of dynamite! That image suggests the greatness of the energy found in authentic Christian witness. It's similar to another dynamic image given by Jesus earlier in his ministry. "Remember this!" Jesus declares in Matthew 17:20, "If you have faith as big as a mustard seed, you can say to this hill [mountain], 'Go from here to there!' and it will go. You could do anything!" (TEV). Christian witness can be so potent, Jesus suggests, it can move even the mightiest of obstacles.

In 1988 the Russian Orthodox Church celebrated its millennium, one thousand years of existence. The church took hold among the Russian people in 988 when St. Vladimir encouraged the growth and expansion of Christianity. Since the Russian Revolution in 1917, Christians in the Soviet Union have faced difficult times. Yet despite unbelievable opposition and sometimes rigorous persecution, the church in the Soviet Union prospers. A seventy-year-old national policy of atheism has not crushed the faith of Soviet Christians. On the contrary, Soviet leaders today look to Christians as models of morality in a nation plagued by alcoholism, drug addiction, prostitution, theft, and indifference.[5]

Such long-suffering endurance is characteristic of the power of the gospel and the scriptures. The story is told of a minister who sent a number of his books off to be rebound. When the books came back, he was surprised that the bookbinder had simply printed the initials of each title on the spine of the book. Imagine his further surprise when he came across one book with the initials "T.N.T." Opening it up, he discovered it was a copy of the New Testament. The New Testament, he reflected, is truly T.N.T.![6]

I was licensed to the ministry in 1971. Boldly (or foolishly) I stood before my church family and explained that preaching was not one of my spiritual gifts and I didn't want to be pressured to preach. At that point I assumed that my calling was to youth work and visitation.

Sometime later the church's youth advisor asked me if I would conduct a Sunday morning worship time with our youth. It was to take place at a retreat to be held at a public campground. That sounded manageable enough, so I agreed.

What she didn't tell me, though, was that I was to conduct the worship service for the youth and the entire campground! After receiving that news–literally at the eleventh hour on Saturday evening–I considered my options. I finally realized that if there was to be a sermon the next day something beyond my own resources would have to do it. And so I prayed. Nervously but with assurance I went to sleep.

The next day a sermon was delivered. I am confident that a power beyond myself guided me through it. I credit that power to the Holy Spirit. It's been seventeen years since then, but that experience remains vivid in my mind. Through all the ups and downs of ministry I still hold on to a very real faith that it is God's power that carries me on.

These illustrations remind us that God has made the Holy Spirit available–not only to the early church, but to the contemporary church too. Yes, we have been called to share the vision of the kingdom. Yes, it is an awesome task. But we have the promise of power, a power, a dunamis, that can move mountains and overcome the mightiest of obstacles.

This power shakes things up and changes people. It can even help us overcome our fears–fears of reaching out and inviting persons to come and see the wonders of our God.

Witness

The reason Jesus promises the power of the Holy Spirit is to enable us to be witnesses for him. We learned that the word witness literally means "one who remembers and can tell about something." In its most radical sense it also means "martyr." Such a concept seems foreign to the contemporary church, but is it?

Bill Bosler was pastor of the First Church of the Brethren in Miami, Florida. He had a deep sense of calling to that congregation and its community. During eight years of ministry his congregation grew from 12 to 70 persons. It changed from an all-white congregation to a rainbow of Haitians, Puerto Ricans, Salvadorans, Jamaicans, Anglos, and American blacks. The congregation began an active and intentional outreach to the community. Countless persons were housed and fed, many by the Boslers personally.

On December 22, 1986, Bill Bosler was murdered. He was stabbed to death by one of the very persons he sought to reach. The congregation in Miami lost a deeply-loved pastor. His family lost a cherished husband and father.

But amazingly, Bill Bosler's witness continued even in death. Honoring his long-standing commitment to peace and reconciliation, Bill's family asked that his murderer not be given the death sentence. Such a fate—even for a murderer—would be a denial of all that Bill Bosler stood for. The peace of Christ, not the violence of the world, was the testimony of his life.[7] Bill Bosler is a contemporary martyr, one who remembered and testified, even unto death. Both his life and his death demonstrate the possibilities for powerful witness in a darkened world.

It is unlikely that many of us will be called to witness to the point of giving our very lives. But all of us are called to "die" to parts of our present lifestyle in order to become more effective witnesses. Do the people who know us think of us as ones "who remember and tell about something," specifically the "something" found in the compassion, forgiveness, and peace of Jesus Christ?

We are called to witness to the remarkable gospel offered by Jesus Christ. We are called to announce the reign of God and the good news of God's kingdom. We are called to invite others to know the life and convictions of the family of faith.

All power on high is available to energize us toward this mission. The risen Christ is behind us and before us. The Holy Spirit has come upon us. Jerusalem, Judea, Samaria, the whole world awaits!

Responding to the Scriptures

1. What is it for you to wait for the Holy Spirit? How does (or has) Pentecost happen(ed) for you?

2. What events or experiences can you share which demonstrate for you the power of the Holy Spirit in your life?

3. In what events of your life has the Spirit of God brought about your witness to Jesus Christ?

4. What is it like to attempt to have the power of Jesus Christ or to witness to Jesus Christ without the spirit?

5. Is the spirit moving mountains now? With dynamite? What is happening?

6. (To be completed after the group discussion.) My learnings from this session are ...

Preparation for the Next Session

1. Pray daily for yourself and the other participants.

2. Read and consider the scripture text and content in Chapter 2.

3. Complete REFLECTING ON THE SCRIPTURES and RESPONDING TO THE SCRIPTURES in Chapter 2.

2

Beginning
Where We Are

Purpose

- To recognize that inviting and welcoming others begins with those we know best

Reading the Scriptures

Read and consider Acts 1:8; Deuteronomy 6:1-9.
My first responses to these passages are . . .

Exploring the Scriptures

Acts 1:8

Do you remember as a child tossing a pebble into a pond or lake and watching the concentric circles move out from the center point? This is the image Luke evokes in Acts 1:8.

God's empowered witnesses move out on their mission in a progressive fashion. They begin at the point where the pebble first enters the water, at home in Jerusalem. From there the message expands regionally into the surrounding area of Judea. Next it travels north into Samaria, an area populated by persons considered to be "half-breeds." Tirelessly the witness keeps expanding until the message of Jesus Christ touches the farthest points of the then-known world.

For the moment, however, our focus is on our own Jerusalem and Judea, on ways to begin witnessing where we are. Along with home and familiar ground, Jerusalem as a symbol suggests "foundation." Contrary to the traditional idea that "Jerusalem" means "city of peace," it actually means "foundation of Shalem," Shalem being an ancient semitic god. The root yrh from which Jer- comes (as in Jerusalem) is used in Job to mean laying a cornerstone.[1] In its most basic sense then, beginning in Jerusalem is not just starting on familiar ground. It is also laying a foundation, a cornerstone for future effectiveness as witnesses.

Deuteronomy 6:1-9

Along with Acts 1:8, a pivotal scripture for understanding our beginning role as witnesses is Deuteronomy 6:1-9. These verses are set in the context of the giving of the Ten Commandments. After admonishing the people of Israel to obey the commandments "as long as you live" (v. 2, TEV) and to "love the Lord your God with all your heart, with all your soul, and with all your strength" (v. 5, TEV), Yahweh declares: "Never forget these commands that I am giving you today. Teach them to your children. Repeat them when you are at home and when you are away, when you are resting and when you are working" (vv. 6-7, TEV).

These words of Moses signal a significant change in the way God speaks to God's people. Up to this point God has tended to communicate through bold, dramatic historical events such as the miracles of the Exodus. Now the message of Yahweh is to be passed along from person to person, informed by written revelation (i.e., the Ten Commandments).

The passing along or teaching of truth is to be done with some intensity. Literally the Hebrew word for teach, shana, in verse seven means to prick in, inculcate, impress upon repeatedly.[2]

This persistent, determined style is further confirmed in the words that follow. God's message is to be taught in formal instruction "when you are at home," even when the family travels, "when you are away," and with visual aids—"tie them on your arms and wear them on your foreheads" (v. 8) and "write them on the doorposts of your houses and on your gates" (v. 9).

Along with conveying general guidelines for passing on God's truth, these verses hold a special message for parents. Commenting on Deuteronomy 6:7-9, Lawrence O. Richards has noted:

> Parents are viewed as the primary communicators of faith's life to their children. The unique relationship between parents and children ... provides the ideal context in which communication of revealed truth and its life impact can take place.[3]

The evangelistic learning from this statement is significant. The closer the relationship between witness and hearer (parent to child, brother to brother, sister to sister, friend to friend) the greater the possibility for conveying the message of God's love, hope, and caring.

The Bible contains many examples of this principle at work. For example, the Apostle Paul describes the part family plays in the faith of his young co-worker, Timothy: "I remember the sincere faith you have, the kind of faith that your grandmother Lois and your mother Eunice also had. I am sure that you have it also" (2 Tim. 1:5 TEV).

Brother-to-brother witness is illustrated by the example of Andrew: "At once he [Andrew] found his brother Simon and told him, 'We have found the Messiah'" (John 1:41 TEV).

Philip illustrates possibilities for faith-sharing among friends: "Philip found Nathanael and told him, 'We have found the one whom Moses wrote about in the book of the Law and whom the prophets also wrote about. He is Jesus son of Joseph, from Nazareth'" (John 1:45 TEV).

The story of the Samaritan woman at the well demonstrates the impact our witness often has among co-workers and neighbors: "Many of the Samaritans in that town believed in Jesus because the woman had said, 'He told me everything I have ever done'" (John 4:39 TEV).

The scriptures are clear. The ministry of inviting and welcoming others to faith begins right where we are, with those closest to us. As we begin with our Jerusalem and Judea, we lay a foundation, a base for future witnessing efforts. A cornerstone is established around which we expand and build our outreach.

Reflecting on the Scriptures

1. What is the "Great Commandment" of Jesus? (See Matthew 22:37.)

2. How does the work of repeating this Great Commandment in various ways, such as putting it up on door posts, cooperate with the work of the Spirit?

3. What other scriptures (if any) do these passages bring to mind?

Applying the Scriptures

Identifying Our Jerusalem and Judea

Contemporary church growth literature supports the Biblical call to begin our witness at home in our Jerusalem and Judea. Numerous studies have confirmed that 70 to 90 percent of all new church members initially come to a congregation because of the invitation of a friend, relative, or acquaintance.[4]

There are numerous reasons for the effectiveness of such an approach. Perhaps the most obvious are familiarity and trust. People are prone to respond to us when they know us. Part of that knowing comes from seeing us in action. When persons are in a position to hear our words of faith and observe those words in every day practice, our witness has greater authenticity.

It's amazing how fleshing out a concept brings it alive for folks. The story is told of a frustrated college student who had been assigned a long book to read.

> After a few pages she could see nothing of worth in it. It was slow reading, poorly written, and about a subject that did not interest her in the least. Boring, boring, boring.
>
> The author, who happened to be a member of the faculty at that school, attended a social gathering at which the student was also present. She met him. He was young, handsome, and engaging—a wonderful conversationalist with exciting ideas.
>
> That night when she was back in her room, she picked up the book he had authored. She began to read. To her surprise it suddenly seemed exciting, very readable, something she could not put down. For her the word had become flesh. A warm, personable human being had brought dry words to life.[5]

So too as we witness to those closest to us, dry words come to life. The word becomes flesh. The gospel comes alive for folks.

"But," you say, "reaching out to my co-worker (spouse, child, neighbor, etc.) is hard. I've tried, but I get nowhere." There is no question that witnessing in our Jerusalem and Judea may be the most effective form of evangelism, but it can also be very discouraging.

Perhaps our morale will be boosted if we realize that few people come into the community of faith instantaneously. In fact, one research group has discovered that "persons who become active Christians have been invited or had the Good News shared with them an average of eight times before they committed themselves."[6]

Such research is consistent with the image found in Deuteronomy 6:7-9 of the truth of God being passed along or taught repeatedly. Persons seldom respond to our initial efforts to guide them towards faith. Over and over and over again, we need to beckon them toward the love and lordship of Christ.

Merlin Garber, a noted pastor and evangelist, recounts his struggles in helping a particular congregation to grow. People seemed to like him as a person and were attracted to his preaching; but they would join other churches. Asking around, he soon discovered why. The other pastors were more diligent and persistent in actually inviting newcomers to join their congregations.

That learning led Garber to compare witnessing to courtship. Over an extended period of time—and with many expressions of interest and love—we are called literally to woo persons into the kingdom of God.[7]

Dropping the Pebble

In his landmark book, Christian Mass Movements in India, J. Wascom Pickett tells the story of Ditt. Living in the 1870s, Ditt was a little, dark, lame man of the untouchable Chuhra caste. After his conversion and against the advice of the missionaries, he immediately returned to his village, his people, and his trade. In spite of a period of rejection, Ditt persevered and loved his people.

Three months after his baptism he reappeared at the missionary station and presented his wife, his daughter, and two neighbors. Ditt had taught them what he knew; they professed their faith in Jesus Christ; and now they had walked thirty miles to be baptized! Six months later Ditt brought four other men to be baptized.

Ditt's occupation of buying and selling hides took him to many villages. Wherever he went, he told his fellow Chuhras of Christ. Many abused him, but an increasing number heard him patiently, and before long groups here and there made Christian commitments. "In the eleventh year after Ditt's conversion," Pickett reports, "more than five hundred Chuhras were received into the Church. By 1900, more than half of these . . . people . . . had been converted, and by 1915 all but a few hundred members of the caste professed the Christian faith."[8] The story of Ditt illustrates the power of reaching others through existing networks of relationships. As his life touched that of his wife, daughter, friends, and co-workers, a wide range of persons came to know Christ and Christ's community.

Our witness will probably never match Ditt's. Nevertheless great things can happen as we begin to share the reality of Jesus Christ from parent to child, friend to friend, neighbor to neighbor, co-worker to co-worker.

It is "a holy privilege," George Hunter writes, "to offer countless people the call to discipleship and the means of transformed identity and liberated life in Christ. So I invite you . . . to add extensively to the shelves of biographies of grace."[9]

I do as well. Think of the persons around you who don't know Christ and the fellowship of Christ's church. Think of persons right at hand whom you could invite to come and see the community of faith.

Drop your pebble. Start your witness. Discover your Jerusalem. Reach out. Begin where you are, now.

Responding to the Scriptures

1. Who are the people who have meaningfully communicated the faith to you?

2. In what ways did they communicate the faith to you?

3. If faith were contagious, who would most likely "catch" it from you? Why?

4. Who would be least likely to "catch" faith from you? Why?

5. How do you keep the "Great Commandment" before yourself?

6. Are the words of this commandment "written upon your heart"?

7. Are they written upon the heart of your congregation?

8. How are they taught to the children?

9. (To be completed after the group discussion.) My learnings from this session are . . .

Preparation for the Next Session

1. Pray daily for yourself and other participants.

2. Thank at least one person who has meaningfully communicated faith to you.

3. Read and consider the scripture text and content in Chapter 3.

4. Complete REFLECTING ON THE SCRIPTURES and RESPONDING TO THE SCRIPTURES in Chapter 3.

3

In Samaria?

Purpose

- To realize that we are sometimes called to share Christ's gospel with those who are different and "despised"

Reading the Scriptures

Read and consider Acts 1:8; 2 Kings 17; John 4:1-42.
My first responses to these passages are . . .

Exploring the Scriptures

Acts 1:8

Thinking once again of our image of the dropped pebble and the concentric circles, we now move from Jerusalem and Judea to Samaria. Our circle of influence and witness is ever widening.

The region of Samaria lies sandwiched between Judea to the south and Galilee to the north. For Jews wishing to travel between Judea and Galilee there are two options. They can go through Samaria or cross the Jordan River and travel north on the east side of the river. Because of the long-standing hatred between Jews and Samaritans, most Jews choose to travel the longer route outside of Samaria.[1]

To the Jewish apostles, Christ's call to go to Samaria is a shock. To witness in Jerusalem and Judea (i.e., at home) is one thing, but to tell the good news in Samaria—unthinkable!

2 Kings 17

The long-standing hostility between the Jews and the Samaritans begins in 2 Kings 17. The Jewish people are divided into two kingdoms: the Northern Kingdom (Israel) and the Southern Kingdom (Judah), each with its own king.

Israel, the Northern Kingdom, has fallen to the conquering Assyrians (721 b.c.). The Assyrians have deported many of Israel's leaders, taking them to the land of the Medes, a section of the Assyrian Empire lying east of the Zagros mountains. Those left behind lack the leadership skills needed for rebellion.

In the course of time the Assyrians bring people of many nationalities to live with the Northern Kingdom Jews. Inevitably, intermarrying takes place. The once "pure" Jewish lineage is corrupted by "foreign" blood.

In 586 b.c. Judah, the Southern Kingdom, also falls to conquerors. Many Jews are exiled to Babylon. Unlike the experience of their northern neighbors, however, these Jews are able to hold stubbornly to their Jewish identity. They remain "clean," untainted by foreign influence.

Years later, Persian King Cyrus allows these Southern Kingdom Jews to return to their homeland, Judea. Upon their return they establish as their top priority the rebuilding of the Jerusalem temple. Some Jews from the north, which is now called Samaria, come to Jerusalem and the Jewish leader Zerubbabel. "Let us join you in building the

Temple," they exclaim. "We worship the same God you worship" (Ezra 4:2 TEV).

The Jewish leaders, however, snub the Samaritans. "We don't need your help," they reply (v. 3). Why? Because the Samaritan "Jews" are half-breeds. They have intermarried. Their bloodline is impure, permanently tainted.

Eventually, the Samaritans build their own temple on Mount Gerizim. This fuels tensions even more, and in 129 b.c. the Jews of the Southern Kingdom attack and destroy the Samaritan temple.

John 4:1-42

Through the course of biblical history, the hatred between Samaritans and Jews continues to escalate. By Jesus' day it is at a feverish pitch. Nevertheless, Jesus confronts its reality head-on. In John 4 we find Jesus traveling directly through Samaria (instead of taking the longer eastern route) to the city of Sychar. While the disciples go and buy lunch, Jesus rests at a well and encounters a woman.

Several aspects of this account are relevant to the ministry of invitation and faith-sharing. Given the theme of this chapter, however, we focus directly on the "Samaritan factor." How does Jesus react to this "half-breed?" Does he despise her? Does he act superior and haughty? Does he ridicule her because she is different?

The answer is, of course, no. Compassionately, Jesus witnesses to this woman, in spite of her questionable lineage and sordid past. "Jesus said to her, 'Give me a drink of water. . . .' The woman answered, 'You are a Jew, and I am a Samaritan—so how can you ask me for a drink?' Jesus answered, 'If you only knew what God gives. . . . '" (John 4:7-10 TEV).

The Biblical message is clear. Jesus breaks down barriers. To him, this despised Samaritan, this traditional enemy, is not an enemy at all. Rather Jesus sees her as a person needing ministry and the challenge of the gospel.

The impact of Jesus' witness continues with the call to Samaria in Acts 1:8 and the call for inclusiveness in other situations confronting the early church. Reflecting on the struggle of the early Christians of Jewish descent to accept Gentiles, Paul recalls the spirit of Christ: "For Christ himself has brought us peace by making Jews and Gentiles one people. With his own body he broke down the wall that separated them and kept them enemies" (Eph. 2:14 TEV).

Reflecting on the Scriptures

1. In what ways does Jesus' description of the new way of worshiping mark a major change between the Old Testament and New?

2. What role does the Spirit have in these passages?

3. What other scriptures (if any) do these passages bring to mind?

Applying the Scriptures

What Is My Samaria?

In the excellent Public Broadcasting System documentary, "Faces of the Enemy," researcher Sam Keen explores the way nations work to depersonalize their enemies in order to make war more palatable. He comments, "Before we make war, even before we make weapons, we make an idea of the enemy." The production points out that nonviolent persons will seldom commit violent acts unless the enemy is first portrayed as less than human. One veteran of the Vietnam war is quoted as saying, "A soldier's most powerful weapon is not his rifle; it is his idea of enemy." Sam Keen concludes, "The image of the enemy . . . is society's most powerful weapon."[2]

When we consider the long-standing tensions between Jews and Samaritans, we realize the truth of Keen's words. Though these two peoples share the same heritage, worship the same God, and believe at least part of the same faith story, enmity grows between them.

Why? Largely it occurs because Samaritans are cast in a negative light. They are thought to be unclean and tainted, which leads to the feeling that they are different, even strange, which leads to the idea that they are the enemy.

Who have we cast in a negative light? Some foreign land, a neighbor down the street, a particular political candidate, a member of our Sunday school class? Who is "tainted" in our minds? Who is the enemy?

Jesus' call to Samaria teaches us to pay attention to the people around us. After all, Samaria is just north of Jerusalem and Judea. Jesus seems to be saying, we are called first to encounter the enemies within our reach.

Robert Tuttle tells of sibling rivalry among his children. After a vigorous disagreement, his three kids retired, only to be aroused at 2:00 a.m. by a terrific thunderstorm. Hearing an unusual noise upstairs, Tuttle called and asked what was going on. A little voice answered, "We are all in the closet forgiving each other."[3]

Facing our Samarias means facing those we know best.

Had to Go

The gospel writer's words in John 4:4 (TEV) are intriguing: "On his way there [to Galilee] he had to go through

Samaria." The phrase "had to go" means "it was necessary." Why did Jesus have to go through Samaria? Obviously it was not because there was no alternative route. As we have already seen, the eastern itinerary was used by class-conscious Jews on a regular basis. No, Jesus "had to go through Samaria" for other reasons. As Roger Fredrikson has commented, Jesus had to go because of "an inner constraint of love and obedience."[4]

We too are called to go to our Samarias out of deep convictions, convictions rooted in Christ calling us towards compassion, caring, and the breaking down of barriers. Such conviction and drive will sometimes lead us away from the status quo. As we listen to voices deep within, we will risk being different. In a world filled with enemies, we will dare to work for peace; in a world crammed with affluence, we will dare to embrace the least, the lost, and the lonely.

Becky Pippert tells of meeting a young man named Bill in Portland, Oregon.

> He was brilliant and looked like he was always pondering the esoteric. His hair was always mussy, and in the entire time I knew him, I never once saw him wear a pair of shoes. Rain, sleet or snow, Bill was always barefoot. While he was attending college he had become a Christian. At this time a well-dressed, middle-class church across the street from the campus wanted to develop more of a ministry to the students. They were not sure how to go about it, but they tried to make them feel welcome. One day Bill decided to worship there. He walked into this church, wearing his blue jeans, T-shirt and of course no shoes. People looked a bit uncomfortable, but no one said anything. So Bill began walking down the aisle looking for a seat. The church was quite crowded that Sunday, so as he got down to the front pew and realized that there were no

seats, he just squatted on the carpet–perfectly acceptable behavior at a college fellowship, but perhaps unnerving for a church congregation. The tension in the air became so thick one could slice it.

Suddenly an elderly man began walking down the aisle toward the boy. Was he going to scold Bill? My friends who saw him approaching said they thought, "You can't blame him. He'd never guess Bill is a Christian. And his world is too distant from Bill's to understand. You can't blame him for what he's going to do."

As the man kept walking slowly down the aisle, the church became utterly silent, all eyes were focused on him, you could not hear anyone breathe. When the man reached Bill, with some difficulty he lowered himself and sat down next to him on the carpet. He and Bill worshiped together on the floor that Sunday. I was told there was not a dry eye in the congregation.[5]

That's what happens as we begin to relate to our Samaritans. People are amazed. In a world of class distinctions, sophistication, and "enemies," it's an unusual sight.

Who are the Samaritans we exclude from our lives and congregations? Persons of color? The handicapped? The poor? "Messy" youth?

Go ahead, invite and welcome such persons. Take the risky route and move into Samaria. Encounter persons who are different and even alien. Dare to include all of God's people!

Responding to the Scriptures

1. Tell the story of how an "unacceptable" person enriched your life.

2. With what groups of "Samaritans" could you have personal contact?

3. Are there inaccurate images that you have about these "Samaritans" which falsely make them out to be your enemy?

4. Are there ways in which differences (i.e., religious directions, competition for resources, values, etc.) are so great that you and the "Samaritans" are real enemies?

5. How could you find ways you could be Christ-centered in your relationship with these "Samaritans"?

6. When have you experienced forgiveness?

7. In what areas do you need to ask forgiveness before you seek a personal relationship with any of these "Samaritans"?

8. In what areas do you need to practice forgiveness before you seek a personal relationship with any of these "Samaritans"?

9. What do you have to offer your enemy?

10. (To be completed following discussion) My learnings from this session are ...

Preparation for the Next Session

1. Pray daily for yourself and the other participants.

2. Pray for your "enemies" by name.

3. Read and consider the scripture text and content in Chapter 4.

4. Complete REFLECTING ON THE SCRIPTURES and RESPONDING TO THE SCRIPTURES in Chapter 4.

4

To the Ends of the Earth

Purpose

- To hear Christ's call for a passionate witness which reaches persons anywhere at any cost

Reading the Scriptures

Read and consider Acts 1:8; Luke 15:1-10.
My first responses to these passages are . . .

Exploring the Scriptures

Acts 1:8

Recall once again the image of the pebble dropped into a pond. Concentric circles form, eventually moving farther and farther away from the center point where the pebble first entered the water.

So goes our witness. After a period of time our outreach needs to "go the distance," venturing into places that are not within convenient reach. You will receive power, Jesus says in Acts 1:8, to witness in Jerusalem and Judea (to family, friends, and people of like culture), in Samaria (to the "enemy" and those who are "different"), and eventually to the ends of the earth (to persons everywhere and of all kinds).

The challenge in Acts 1:8 to witness even to the ends of the earth parallels the command in Matthew 28:19 (TEV), to "Go, then, to all peoples everywhere and make them my disciples." The words "all peoples" is a literal rendering of the Greek phrase panta ta ethne. Normally this phrase is translated using the word "nations" ("Go therefore and make disciples of all nations. . . . " Matt. 28:19). However, this is incorrect. As Jesus gives the command to reach all peoples, he is not thinking of modern nation-states such as India or the United States. Rather, he is thinking of the families of humankind—the various tongues, tribes, castes and lineages of the world.[1]

Luke 15:1-10

Exploring Luke's gospel, we find additional evidence of Jesus' concern for reaching all peoples. In Luke 15, for example, it is clear that Jesus has a passion for "finding" individuals outside of the community of faith. Two stories in particular illustrate this concern: the parable of the lost sheep (Luke 15:4-7) and the parable of the lost coin (Luke 15:8-10).

The setting for both stories is the same. Jesus is surrounded by opposition and controversy. The Jewish religious officials of his day (the scribes and Pharisees) are visibly upset. Jesus is spending time with outcasts and common folk (tax collectors and people of the land), and the religious leaders are disgusted at such irregular behavior.

The Pharisees do not seek the salvation of "the people of the land" (or of the tax collectors for that matter). Instead, they pray that the nation be rid of such "uncleanness." William Barclay quotes pharisaic regulations:

> When a man is one of the People of the Land, entrust no money to him, take no testimony from him, trust him with no secret, do not appoint him guardian of an orphan, do not make him the custodian of charitable funds, do not accompany him on a journey.[2]

It is in this hostile context that Jesus tells the parable of the lost sheep. The Pharisees and scribes undoubtedly find his words grating as he describes a God who goes out of his way to find stray sheep, the least and the lost.

Their consciences must be pricked by the memory of Ezekiel's words, "Woe to the shepherds of Israel who only take care of themselves! Should not shepherds take care of the flock?" (Ezek. 34:2 NIV). Or the words of the prophet Zechariah, "I have put a shepherd in charge of my flock, but he does not help the sheep . . . nor does he look for the lost, or heal those that are hurt" (Zech. 11: 16 TEV).

If the parable of the lost sheep is not enough, Jesus continues with the parable of the lost coin in Luke 15:8-10. While different in its imagery, this story reinforces the picture of a God who is relentless in his search for anyone anywhere who is outside of his realm, who is lost. The coin mentioned in this parable is probably a Greek drachma, a silver coin worth about 44 cents today or a day's wages in New Testament times.[3] For most people, especially a single woman, the loss of a day's wages is a tragic occurrence, jeopardizing the ability to put food on the table. Note then the vigor and diligence of the woman's search for the lost coin. "She lights a lamp, sweeps her house, and looks carefully everywhere until she finds it" (Luke 15:8 TEV). She combs her dirt floor compulsively, her eyes straining in the dim light to catch a glimpse of the coin.

This, Jesus says, is how God searches the world for those who lack relationship with him. He looks everywhere, compulsively, shining his light into the darkness. Each person is valuable and precious. As William Barclay has noted, "No Pharisee had ever dreamed of God like that."[4]

Reflecting on the Scriptures

1. How many different ways can you find to interpret the identities of the "sheep" and the "lost coin"?

2. Who would the Pharisees and scribes interpret the "sheep" and "lost coin" to be?

3. What other scriptures (if any) do these passages bring to mind?

Applying the Scriptures

Treasure

One of my valued possessions is a very old copy of volume five of Matthew Henry's Commentary. The pages are yellow and brittle, the spine is held together by masking tape. Most people looking at this book would consider it a worthless, tattered volume. But to me it is a treasured possession. Inside the front cover is the signature of C. H. Steerman, my great, great grandfather, a Church of the Brethren minister. A close friend recently gave me this volume. It is the only tangible remembrance I have of an esteemed and valued member of my family.

Can you think of a similar possession, something insignificant in the eyes of others, yet of great value to you?

Often in the rush of this world, persons are viewed as insignificant. This is especially true of persons who lack power, material wealth, or visible talent. They appear worn and tattered. The good news of the gospel is that Jesus Christ seeks out such persons! The very individuals who are rejected or passed over by the world are esteemed by God.

The central truth of the scriptures is that God values each of us. No matter where we are, what we do, or how tattered we have become, God keeps reaching for us. Tony Campolo, the noted author and speaker, describes God's love for all in vivid terms. "It's like this," he declares, "if God had a wallet, your picture would be in it!"

Imagine a God who values each one of us that much. No wonder the scriptures picture God leaving the ninety-nine and looking for the one lost sheep and scurrying through a house searching for one lost coin. From a divine perspective, every human being is greatly treasured.

Passion

When you value people, you want to reach them. The shepherd in Luke 15 does not look casually for the lost sheep. Rather he looks "for the one that got lost until he finds it" (v. 4 TEV). Or in the story of the lost coin the woman "looks carefully everywhere until she finds it" (v. 8 TEV).

Passion for reaching persons is essential in our ministry of inviting and welcoming others. In a sense we have no other choice. We have discovered in the message of Jesus Christ amazing good news! Alienation and loneliness are not the only options in life. Through the love of God and the fellowship of the faith community, persons can be found!

Such news, the Scriptures tell us, is to be shouted "from the housetops" (Matthew 10:27 NEB). In the Sermon on the Mount, Jesus reminds us that "You are like light for the whole world . . . No one lights a lamp to put it under a bowl. . . . In the same way your light must shine before people, so that they will . . . give praise to your Father in heaven." (Matthew 5:14-16 TEV).

Ends of the Earth

The activity of shouting from the housetops and being light for the world sends us into the world, or as Acts 1:8 notes, to the ends of the earth. A growing passion for inviting others to faith requires a growing vision. It involves a new willingness to fathom the far-reaching love of Jesus Christ. It causes us to take a new look at "foreign lands," at unfamiliar places and people.

In 1984 Raymond J. Bakke, then a professor at Northern Baptist Theological Seminary, spoke to 18,000 college students at Urbana '84, a missions conference. "Stop running away from the cities," he pleaded. Continuing, he noted that of the two billion "unreached" persons in the world, half of them are living in cities.

> The world is growing at the rate of more than one metropolitan Chicago a month. Each of the world-class cities will double in size in the next 15 years. A city the size of Seattle is born within Mexico City alone every year.[5]

Yet, Bakke concludes, the church is out of touch with the city. In the urban setting, Christian folks are often viewed as irrelevant and out of date. Rather than moving toward urban needs and ministry, the church is at a standstill or, worse yet, moving in the other direction.

Perhaps "the ends of the earth" are not as distant as we first imagined. Perhaps the "foreign" places and people we need to venture towards are already in view.

Christ died for the whole world, rural and urban, local and distant. Familiar and unfamiliar. No matter where they are located, we need to reach all those outside the community of faith. Inviting and welcoming others challenges us to expand our vision and to see beyond the safe and convenient. Ultimately, faithful outreach calls us to go where we've never gone before. It summons us to explore some new "land" looking for one last lost sheep, searching for one last lost coin, longing for those yet to be found!

Responding to the Scriptures

1. Do you find other persons to be "treasures" in your life?

2. Are they so valuable that you would, for a time, abandon the safe relationships of your life to passionately go and "find" the "lost sheep" for Christ?

3. How could your passion for the lost be raised in intensity?

4. How about the passion within your congregation?

5. Can you see yourself as "shepherding" another person?

6. How does your congregation "shepherd" the lost back into the flock?

7. Under what conditions would you expand your witness into a "foreign land"?

8. (To be completed following discussion) My learnings from this session are...

Preparation for the Next Session

1. Pray daily for yourself and the other participants.

2. Read and consider the scripture text and content in Chapter 5.

3. Complete REFLECTING ON THE SCRIPTURES and RESPONDING TO THE SCRIPTURES in Chapter 5.

4. Complete RESPONDING TO THE CALL FOR ACTION.

Responding to the Call for Action

1. The things I have learned which are calling me to invite and welcome are...

2. The persons I feel called to invite and welcome are...

3. In the next four weeks I will invite and welcome...

4. My invitations will include a message of...

I _____ will
ask _____ to help
me be accountable for the above actions.

5

The Receptive Moment

Purpose

- To affirm that there are moments in life when persons are more ready and willing to accept invitations to faith

Reading the Scriptures

Read and consider Acts 8:26-40.
My first responses to this passage are . . .

Exploring the Scriptures

Along with defining the scope of our witness, the scriptures also provide practical strategies for carrying out that witness. Acts 8:2-40 is a case in point. Through the story of Philip's encounter with the Ethiopian eunuch we discover an important first step in implementing our ministry of inviting and welcoming others–sensing right, receptive moments.

The two principle characters in our scripture text are of course Philip and the Ethiopian. The Philip mentioned here is not Philip the Apostle, one of Jesus' twelve disciples. Rather he is Philip the Evangelist, an influential leader in the early church who was numbered among the very first deacons (Acts 6).

The Ethiopian is an unnamed, but high-ranking official in charge of the treasury of Candace, queen of the Ethiopians (8:27). He is also a eunuch. Traditionally, a eunuch was a man who for the purposes of serving in a royal household was castrated to make any chance or rumor of sexual impropriety impossible. Unger's Bible Dictionary points out, however, that in Greek the word was used sometimes to describe persons filling important positions without any implication of physical mutilation.[1]

The story begins with the Holy Spirit directing Philip to "Go south to the road that goes from Jerusalem to Gaza" (v. 26 TEV). This route passes through the hilly terrain around Betogabris into an arid region leading to Gaza, a city some thirty miles west and south of Jerusalem.[2]

Philip, however, never reaches Gaza. On his way to that desert city he encounters the Ethiopian. Their meeting probably occurs around noontime. This is inferred from an alternate reading for the word south in verse 26. Literally the word for south (meseembria) means "at noon" or "midday" (see Acts 22:6).[3]

The Ethiopian is returning to his home after a time of worship in Jerusalem. It seems odd that this high official of the Ethiopian government has journeyed to the center of Judaism for a time of spiritual renewal. However, as William Barclay notes:

> In those days the world was full of people who were weary of the many gods and the loose morals of the nations. They came to Judaism and there found the one God and the austere moral standards that gave life meaning.[4]

As Philip comes upon the Ethiopian, the spirit of God gives further guidance, "Go to that chariot and stay near it" (v. 29 NIV). This directive is strongly worded. Literally it means "glue yourself to that chariot!"[5] Running up to the chariot, Philip discovers the Ethiopian reading aloud from a scroll of Isaiah 53. Undoubtedly this government official has found something of value in the life and witness of the Jewish scriptures. The very fact that he is reading from his own scroll (probably purchased in the course of his pilgrimage) indicates the intensity of his quest for the one true God.

Philip opens his conversation with the Ethiopian by asking whether he knows what he is reading. A humorous play on words no doubt breaks the ice. Literally the Greek word for "reading" in verse 30 means "to know again." As Philip is running alongside the Ethiopian's chariot, he is actually questioning "Do you know what you know again?"[6] The Ethiopian admits that he does not know and invites Philip into his chariot.

Philip begins to discuss the meaning of the scripture (Isaiah 53) with his receptive host. The image of a suffering god must intrigue a person of position and power such as the Ethiopian. Philip then proceeds to use this image as a jumping-off point for telling "the good news of Jesus" (v. 35). Eventually, the truth of the Scriptures and the identity of the Messiah come together for the Ethiopian. An "aha" moment takes place. The reality of Jesus Christ comes alive!

The Ethiopian wants to act immediately on his new discovery.

> "Look, here is water. Why shouldn't I be baptized?" And Philip said, "If you believe with all your heart, you may." And he replied, "I believe that Jesus Christ is the Son of God" (Acts 8:36-37 NIV).

The words of Philip in verse 37 are omitted from most translations, since they do not appear in the earliest Greek manuscripts. They are, however, often included in a footnote. These are important words providing insight into the kind of confession of faith used by the early church.

And so the Ethiopian commands his chariot to stop, and both he and Philip go down into the water (v. 38). Philip then proceeds to baptize him. If Philip follows the pattern of the early church, he probably immerses the Ethiopian. The location of the baptism is unknown, but it might take place in a desert oasis pool. The preference, however, of early church leaders is running water, after the pattern of Jesus (see Mark 1:9-10).[7]

Reflecting on the Scriptures

1. What is Philip's motivating force in this story?

2. In the perspective of the first believers an Ethiopian must have been a strange man indeed. How would he, as a new believer, indicate to the young Christian church the breadth of God's grace?

3. What is the significance of the scripture passage the eunuch was reading before Philip approaches?

4. What other scriptures (if any) does this passage, Acts 8:26-40, bring to mind?

Applying the Scriptures

Times of Transition

When are persons most open to our witness? Acts 8:26-40 implies that it is during times of life-change or transition. The Ethiopian eunuch Philip encounters was moving from one world view (the many gods of the Ethiopians) to an entirely different way of life (the one true God of Judaism). This change of philosophy and life-orientation made him highly receptive to the gospel.

Recent church growth findings confirm this biblical principle. It is during times of transition and crisis that persons are most open to our witness. As we look for practical suggestions for beginning the ministry of invitation, this is one of the most important. Rather than moving out in all directions, we are first called to look for strategic "right" moments.

For example, Joe Harding, a United Methodist leader, suggests that we:

> Think especially of persons who are undergoing personal life stresses of some kind. These individuals often find helpful answers to their problems from within the Christian faith—persons who are recently divorced, families with new babies, families which have experienced recent death, families where someone has lost a job or suffered painful business reverses.[8]

Does such an approach seem opportunistic? It certainly may seem so. This is especially true if we begin with our congregation's needs rather than the needs of others. If we are alert to the hurts around us only to pad our church rolls, we have failed. However, if we look for persons in need in order genuinely to meet their need, then we are moving in a Christ-like spirit.

A key assumption here, of course, is that a part of meeting human need is presenting opportunities for persons to discover faith and community. Along with addressing emotional and physical problems, caregivers are ultimately called to address spiritual struggles. Alienation from God, and other people (community) is a fundamental cause of human distress. We are actually doing persons a disservice when we fail to address this very real aspect of their lives.

Sticking Like Glue

The Spirit's call to Philip to "go over to this chariot and join it" (v. 29), to stick to it like glue, reminds us of the intensity of our caring during receptive moments. The open times in person's lives are not necessarily easy times. The ministry of sharing the gospel in crisis often demands a process of "hanging in there" with those who hurt in some way.

Usually once a month I spend all night at a local hospital. I serve as an associate chaplain, available to patients or families of patients who need pastoral care. As with most hospitals, at least 50 percent of those entering our facility claim no church affiliation. Yet I'm always amazed at how open the majority of these "non-affiliated" persons are to words of faith and to the ministry of God's love. Such care, however, involves "hanging in there" with folks through some long periods of waiting and pain. These crisis times make persons more receptive, but also more vulnerable and needy.

Our witness then, in such settings involves a deep investment in person's lives. Mere words are not enough. We are called to be present for extended periods of time, reaching out and caring in tangible ways. Following the example of Philip, we are to "stick like glue."

Being Receptive to the Receptive Moment

Events such as the meeting of Philip and the Ethiopian don't happen by accident. Lloyd Ogilvie writes, "Philip was a man 'full of the Holy Spirit' (Acts 6:3) and therefore could be guided by the Spirit. Preparation for the Gaza road began when the Spirit took possession of his mind long before."[9] Being receptive to the right moment begins with being receptive to the Holy Spirit.

But receptivity is only a start. Along with openness to the Spirit there must be obedience. If Philip had decided that Main Street in Jerusalem was an easier place to witness than on the Gaza road ("I'll probably meet more people there anyway!") or that 5:00 p.m. was a better time to talk to folks than noon ("Most people with any real sense aren't on the road at that hour of the day!"), how different our story would be! But Philip did none of this. When the spirit of God instructed him to rise and go south (Acts 8:26), he obeyed.

It's amazing what occurs when we follow the Spirit's leading. The early church historian Eusebius claims that the Ethiopian in Acts 8 was a man by the name of Indich. As Eusebius reports it, Indich returned to Ethiopia (see Acts 8:39) and founded the Christian church there. Through his strong leadership the good news of the gospel was proclaimed and established in yet another part of the world.[10] Think of your own circle of relationships. Who is waiting to be touched by your life and witness? Who is especially open, vulnerable, and in need? Who has yet to discover the comfort of God and the support of the faith community?

"One thing is clear," a noted church growth author has written, "receptivity wanes as often as it waxes. Like the tide, it comes in and goes out. Unlike the tide, no one can guarantee when it goes out that it will soon come back again."[11]

We are called then to move promptly into opportunities provided by the Spirit, to move into fields ripe unto harvest, to be receptive to receptive moments given and crafted by God!

Responding to the Scriptures

1. A sense of humor is important in faith because

2. When have you been open to the Spirit's leading like Philip?

3. When have you been receptive to hearing the Good News?

4. What impact on your life has that had?

5. How can you tell that another person is receptive to hearing the Good News?

6. When have you needed to "stick like glue" to someone in need?

7. What scripture passage(s) is(are) most helpful to you in explaining what Jesus means to you?

8. How might you be ready to witness to others?

9. Who do you know today who might be receptive to the message?

10. (To be completed after the group discussion.) My learnings from this session are ...

Preparation for the Next Session

1. Pray daily for yourself and the other participants.

2. Begin putting your "action response planning" into effect.

3. Read and consider the scripture text and content in Chapter 6.

4. Complete REFLECTING ON THE SCRIPTURES and RESPONDING TO THE SCRIPTURES in Chapter 6.

6

An Invitation That Fits

Purpose

- To discover that effective invitations are tailored to the unique situation of each individual

Reading the Scriptures

Read and consider Matthew 4:12-22.
My first responses to this passage are . . .

Exploring the Scriptures

Continuing our exploration of ways to carry out a ministry of inviting and welcoming, we turn to Matthew 4:12-22. These verses tell the story of the calling of Peter, Andrew, James, and John. Through this account we discover yet another principle for effective witness: extending invitations "that fit."

The setting of this story is the Sea of Galilee. Also known by the names Chinnereth (today in Israel it is still called Yam Kinneret) and Tiberias, this lake is a heart-shaped body of water 13 miles long and seven and one-half miles wide. On its eastern bank are the high hills of the Golan Heights. When winds come from the west, the hills build up a high pressure area over the lake that keeps the sea calm. However, when the winds shift, severe storms can suddenly buffet the lake's surface.[1] Josephus, the first-century Jewish historian, tells us that the Sea of Galilee was thick with fishing boats. One expedition had no fewer than two hundred and forty fishing vessels sailing from Tarichaea on the western shore of the sea.[2]

Jesus journeys to the area around the Sea of Galilee upon hearing the news that John the Baptist has been arrested (v. 12). John's capture is a sign, a signal to Jesus, that his public ministry must begin. Mindful of the mission before him, he walks along the Sea of Galilee (v. 18). He is probably in the vicinity of Capernaum, his accustomed "home base" during Galilean travels (v. 13). Located on the northern shore of the Sea of Galilee, Capernaum is one of nine cities located around the lake.

As he is walking along he sees two brothers, Simon (who is called Peter) and Andrew his brother "casting a net into the sea—for they were fishermen" (v. 18). By combining the Gospel accounts of Matthew and John, we can conclude that this is not the first time Jesus has met or talked with Simon and Andrew. John 1:35-40 indicates that at an earlier time Andrew was a disciple of John the Baptist at Bethany and spent from four o'clock to sundown in the house where Jesus was living.

How much time has elapsed from that incident to the events recorded in Matthew 4? How much discussion have the two brothers already had concerning the young rabbi Jesus? Has there been any previous talk about leaving their fishing business to become disciples of this man? We sim-

ply don't know. All we can say is that after an initial intro-
duction to Jesus some time passes. And then the Master
reappears, coming to the two brothers with a simple invitation, "Follow me" (V. 19). In response, Peter and Andrew
leave all their fishing gear behind and follow their new
teacher. Not long after that, James and John also respond to
a similar invitation—leaving everything and following the
Christ (vv. 21-22).

To us it may seem strange to leave a good job and family
to follow an itinerant preacher. Actually, these four men
are only doing what is quite common in Jesus's day. Persons often "drop everything" to follow a famous rabbi.

The Greek word for disciple, mathetes, means "pupil."
Disciples in the most literal sense are those who study under the direction of a master teacher. They might study
with a weaver, a physician, or a philosopher.[3] Jesus' style
of discipling, however, is unique. Whereas most rabbis
wait for students to come to them, Jesus seeks out his disciples. In addition, the rabbinic tradition expects students
eventually to "graduate" and leave the influence of their
teacher. For Jesus, participation in his school of discipleship
is for life.[4]

Perhaps the most marked difference, however, is found
in the words "Follow me." Rabbis teach and mingle with
their students, but seldom go beyond intellectual ex-
change. For Jesus, discipleship is not just a matter of
hearing, but doing. Disciples not only listen to Jesus, they
literally follow after him. As A. T. Robertson suggests, Jesus
(in v. 19) is not simply asking Simon, Andrew, James, and
John to be his pupils. He is calling them "to leave their
business and to follow [him] in his travels and work."[5]

Along with the simple invitation "follow me," Jesus also
issues the well-known promise to make his disciples "fishers of men." (v. 19). This phrase indicates something of
Jesus' genius at communication. As he issues an invitation
to come after him, he tailors his summons to the unique
life-work of his potential disciples.

How appropriate to ask a would-be disciple/fisherman to consider catching human beings! Discipleship does not demand a denial of all previous joy and talent; rather the invitation from Jesus is to shift life's focus; to become oriented towards new goals. Augustine said it well, "Fisherman Peter did not lay aside his nets, but changed them."[6]

Reflecting on the Scriptures

1. Was it out of fear that, following John the Baptist's execution, Jesus went into Galilee?

2. Why do you think Matthew used such direct language in describing Jesus' actions towards the first disciples?

3. In what various ways might Jesus' simple message in Matthew 4:17 be interpreted?

4. What other scriptures (if any) does this passage bring to mind?

Applying the Scriptures

Meet Me on My Turf

As we have learned, one of the marks of Jesus' discipling is the initiative he takes in reaching persons. Unlike most rabbis of his day, Jesus seeks out his disciples, spending time "on their turf." To Jesus the discovery of discipleship is more than a classroom exercise. It involves walking, talking, and living with those he hopes to reach. The truth of the Kingdom needs to be seen, sensed, and demonstrated; it needs to be "caught" as well as taught. David Augsburger seems to affirm this method and style of Jesus when he reminds us that the most effective witness is often "with-ness."[7]

Philip Yancey relates the story of a young woman caught in the cruel throes of Lou Gehrig's disease. When he met her she had no appearance of ill health. But it was only a matter of months before the disease, which progresses as nerve cells die, caused her to lose the ability to walk, then to control a wheel chair, and finally to breathe.

Yancey himself offered to her the gospel of Jesus Christ but . . .

> I confess to you readily that the great Christian hopes of eternal life, ultimate healing, and resurrection sounded thin as smoke when held up to someone like Martha. She wanted not angel wings but an arm that did not flop to the side, a mouth that did not drool, and lungs that would not collapse on her.
>
> It became clear that her death was soon. Yet who would care for her at the end?
>
> Only one group in all of Chicago offered the free and loving personal care Martha needed . . . Reba Place Fellowship. That Christian community adopted Martha as a project and volunteered to fulfill her last wishes. They stayed with Martha, listened to her raving and com-

plaints, bathed her, helped her sit up, moved her, and loved her. They were available.[Italics added][8]

As she was nearing death Martha finally accepted the Christ who stood with her in the people of his church. It was their first being where she was, with her, that allowed her to do so.

I Will Make You a Doctor of Souls

As a result of spending time with people, Jesus can make his invitations to faith very specific and very special. As we have already pointed out, the phrase "I will make you fishers of men" (Matt. 4:19 RSV) is an example of Jesus' skill in personalizing calls to discipleship.

If Jesus calls fishermen to become "fishers of men," how does he call a doctor, for example? Does he say, "Come and I will make you a doctor of souls"? Or in the case of a construction worker, does Jesus challenge him or her to be a "rebuilder of lives"?

The point of course is not the exact wording used, but a sensitivity to the unique life of a particular person. Try the exercise yourself. Make a list of some occupations/life situations you are familiar with. How might your Christian witness be uniquely tailored to the world of a computer programmer, a lab technician, a homemaker, an architect? Don't worry about clever images. Do be alert to ways you can personalize your language.

A Variety of Invitations

Because our invitations are to be personal, they will vary not only in language, but in content. It's interesting to note that the gospels record 153 different situations where persons respond to Jesus' message.[9] It follows that there are probably just as many kinds or styles of invitations.

To Simon, Andrew, James, and John, the invitation is to come and follow me (Matt. 4:19). To the rich young ruler it is an invitation to go and "sell all that you own and distrib-

ute the money to the poor" (Luke 18:22). To the woman
caught in adultery the invitation is to go and sin no more
(John 8:11).

Jesus always responds to people with an invitation that
fits just who they are. When I think of my own life, I can
see how my pastor did this. I was a rebellious young teenager who had grown up in the church. Like many young
people in the '60s I was disillusioned with the church and
eager for it to be something more. My frustration was moving me away from the mainstream of church life, and I am
sure a break would have come soon. My pastor invited me
along one night as he took his turn in a community night
ministry. On that evening I saw ministry happen in the
hospital emergency room, the bus station, and the prison.
The invitation was exactly what an idealistic teenager,
who wanted so desperately to see the church really be the
church, needed.

There were many other invitations and milestones
along my faith journey, but it's clear to me that that simple invitation made a very real difference in my life. It fit!

Often we don't feel that we have what it takes to invite
persons into the community of faith. We feel inadequate
and inferior, lacking the right words. We forget however
that faith-sharing is not just supplying "right words" or
some magic formula. As Becky Pippert reminds us:

> When we explain the Christian message, we
> should learn to do so in plain language—we
> hope in fresh and creative ways. Few things
> turn off people faster or alienate them more
> easily than God-talk.[10]

So relax! Use your own language, common language,
practical language. Invite fishermen to become fishers of
people. Remember, the very best invitations are already on
your lips—invitations from the heart, invitations that fit!

Responding to the Scriptures

1. Matthew gives few details about how much information the fishermen had before leaving everything to follow Jesus. What information would you need before you would drop everything and follow him?

2. If Jesus were using your vocation as a basis for an invitation, he might say, "Come, follow me and I will make you..."

3. How would you most simply, describe your faith?

4. By what factors do you determine the content of any particular invitation to Jesus Christ?

5. Please tell a story of a time when your witness connected with your "withness."

6. If you were the pastor, how would you give an altar call to fit your congregation?

7. What is the importance of the work of the Spirit in fitting your witness to another?

8. (To be completed following discussion) My learnings from this session are ...

Preparation for the Next Session

1. Pray daily for yourself and the other participants.

2. Continue with your planned action responses.

3. Read and consider the scripture text and content in Chapter 7.

4. Complete REFLECTING ON THE SCRIPTURES and RESPONDING TO THE SCRIPTURES in Chapter 7.

7

Sharing, But Also Caring

Purpose

- To recognize that we encourage persons to move toward Christ and the Church through a spirit of gracious caring, not force

Reading the Scriptures

Read and consider Luke 19:1-10.
My first responses to this passage are . . .

Exploring the Scriptures

As we move along in our discussion of practical strategies for inviting and welcoming, we come to the matter of attitude or style. An effective witness is a gracious, caring witness. Though hinted at in other chapters, this theme comes alive as we turn now to the story of Jesus and Zacchaeus in Luke 19:1-10.

The setting of this story is Jericho, a well-known biblical city located ten miles northwest of the mouth of the Dead Sea. In Jesus' day Jericho was a major center of commerce. William Barclay notes:

> It lay in the Jordan Valley and commanded both the approach to Jerusalem and the crossings of the river which gave access to the lands east of the Jordan. It had a great palm forest and world-famous balsam groves. The Romans carried its dates and balsam to worldwide trade and fame.[1]

Since 63 b.c. Jews in Jericho and elsewhere had lived under Roman occupation. An especially oppressive part of this occupation was excessive taxation. There were taxes for using the main roads, for using sea harbors, for using the market place, for each wheel on a cart, for each animal pulling a cart, for growing grain (one-tenth of the harvest), for producing wine or oil (one-fifth of the production), and on and on.

As their empire expanded and grew, the Romans discovered that it was harder and harder to collect all these taxes. In an effort to remedy this problem, they decided that local talent could be employed. Jews would be recruited to collect taxes from Jews. An incentive plan helped things along. An area like Jericho was assigned an assessed value. The Romans would proceed to sell the right to collect these taxes to the highest bidder. The successful bidder was then permitted to go out and collect as much as he could. Any amount over and beyond the official assessment became his.

It's not surprising that Jews who participated in this scheme were despised. A common practice was to link tax collectors to sinners and other outcasts. Likewise, it is not surprising that those who befriended tax collectors were also suspect. Jesus discovers this to be the case when he chooses the tax collector Matthew to be one of his disciples (Matt. 9:9-13). He rediscovers this reality when, in the scripture lesson before us, he reaches out to Zacchaeus, a chief tax collector for the Jericho region (Luke 19:2, 7).

Zacchaeus is a prime candidate for some kind of attention. Learning that Jesus is passing through town, he goes out of his way to see him. Because of the press of the crowd and his short stature, Zacchaeus climbs a sycamore tree for a better view (vv. 3-4).

The sycamore tree mentioned in Luke 19 is not the variety we are familiar with in North America. Rather it is a fig tree with branches close to the ground. The figs it produces are of a rather inferior quality usually eaten by the poor who cannot afford more expensive fruits.[2] It is into this "poor man's tree" that the rich Zacchaeus climbs to see Jesus.

Eventually Jesus comes to this place. He looks up to see the strange sight of a wealthy tax collector in a fig tree. Jesus calls out to him, "Hurry down Zacchaeus, because I must stay in your house today" (v. 5 TEV). Zacchaeus immediately responds and welcomes Jesus "with great joy" (v. 6 TEV). The two of them then proceed to Zacchaeus' home.

Luke does not record the details of the conversation that takes place between Zacchaeus and Jesus. Undoubtedly as they eat together and visit, the tax collector experiences love, truth, and challenge. He also experiences a unique kind of care and focused concern. Commenting on the Jesus-Zacchaeus encounter, Bruce Larson says, "When you sit in the presence of the Ultimate Love, you are the agenda."[3]

In the course of their conversation, Zacchaeus promises two things to Jesus. First he says, "I will give half my belongings to the poor" (v. 8 TEV). His second promise is just as dramatic: "If I have cheated anyone, I will pay him back four times as much" (v. 8 TEV). Jewish law required a thief to pay back double what was stolen (Exodus 22:4) unless the crime was especially deliberate and violent. In that case the law required a fourfold payback (Exodus 22:1).[4]

Jesus' response to the repentant Zacchaeus is one of grace and forgiveness. "Today, salvation has come to this house . . . . For the Son of Man came to seek and to save the lost" (vv. 9-10). William Barclay has noted that the word for lost in this scripture does not necessarily mean "doomed"; it may also mean "to be in the wrong place."[5] By his ill-gotten gain, Zacchaeus is in the wrong place spiritually, but under Jesus' influence, he is saved, restored to the right place spiritually.

Reflecting on the Scriptures

1. How did Jesus react to the many sins of Zacchaeus?

2. How important was Zacchaeus' response to Jesus? (See Matthew 21:28-32.)

3. What other scriptures (if any) does this passage bring to mind?

Applying the Scriptures

The Compassionate Witness

Gracious witness is rooted in loving compassion. It's striking that Jesus chooses to go to Zacchaeus' home in spite of the murmuring of the crowds (Luke 19:7). Compelled by the love of God, he reaches out to this despised tax collector in spite of the risks.

Joseph Bayly tells of a young Christian couple living in a changing neighborhood in Detroit. A group of black gang members also lived there. Because of their rowdy lifestyle, the gang members were the bane of the neighborhood. Sometimes they blocked traffic, forcing the couple to go around the block to get to their apartment.

In spite of this obnoxious behavior, the young couple decided to reach out to the group. On Halloween night (of all times), the husband approached some gang members as they hung out on a street corner. He said, "My wife and I'd like to invite you to our apartment for a party." The gang members were surprised but decided to accept the invitation. They came to the party and had a great time. Out of that experience developed a weekly Bible study group and a commitment by one or two gang members to follow Christ.[6]

The real significance of this story is not in its ending, but in its beginning. Christian commitment and discipleship grew out of a couple's willingness to show compassion, love, even vulnerability. The same is true for us. As we are willing to risk loving and caring and serving, a new credibility comes to our witness. Invitations to discipleship make more sense and are more persuasive as they grow out of a spirit of real compassion.

No Force in Religion

Along with compassion, another mark of Jesus' encounter with Zacchaeus is the absence of force or manipulation. The tax collector's conversion comes in the midst of an empathetic conversation with Jesus, not a high-powered lecture.

One cannot force another into a true faith. It is only genuine faith when it has been freely accepted by the individual. And when force has been used, the cause of any true conversion must not be seen as the result of tactics, but rather in spite of those tactics. As Richard Armstrong says when addressing pastors who would be evangelists:

> As soon as one talks about ways of "winning" people, one exposes oneself to the charge of manipulation. Those who resort to deceitful wiles or play upon people's emotions to gain their objectives are guilty as charged. In evangelism the end does not justify the means, nor the means the end! Both the end and the means must be true to and worthy of the gospel of Jesus Christ.[7]

Contemporary church growth research supports the idea that force or manipulation have no place in Christian conversion. In one study 720 individuals were asked what it was like to be on the receiving end of a Christian witness. How would you describe, the study asked, the person who shared faith with you? Was he or she a friend, one who listened and cared; a teacher, one who exhorted and instructed; or a salesman, one who forced and manipulated?

Of those who viewed the "witness" as a friend, 94 percent are currently active in the church. On the other hand, 84 percent of those who viewed the "witness" as a teacher and 71 percent of those who viewed the "witness" as a salesperson, walked away from the Christian faith.[8] What are the implications? Lecturing or pushing people toward the things of God simply does not work. It's the gentle touch, not the forceful shove, that moves persons towards the Kingdom.

We live in an ungracious world. Life is difficult and sends people scrambling. Some persons are "up a tree," caught in affluence, greed, materialism, and pride. Like Jesus we are to find the Zacchaeuses among us and give a gracious hand. The world is weary of high-pressure tactics and hard sell; what is longed for is a witness that is patient, long-suffering, and caring.

Look around. People are waiting to be invited out of their trees. Reach up and lend a hand, not forcefully or arrogantly, but with the grace and compassion of God.

Responding to the Scriptures

1. What would happen to you if you did accept a "high pressure" invitation to faith?

2. What does it mean for Jesus to say that Zacchaeus was "lost"? Isn't that a bit too judgmental for us to say about anyone else?

3. When do you feel "lost"?

4. When are you "lost"?

5. What other persons seem "lost" to you?

6. What do you believe to be the best way to lift another person up so that they might see Jesus?

7. Can you tell the story of a time when you have lifted up another so that they could see Jesus? What was the role of the Spirit in this event?

8. Have you ever felt it necessary to pay back four-fold? Why? If not, why not?

9. (To be completed following discussion) My learnings from this session are...

Preparation for the Next Session

1. Pray daily for yourself and the other participants.

2. Pray by name for those who seem lost.

3. Read and consider the scripture text and content in Chapter 8.

4. Complete REFLECTING ON THE SCRIPTURES and RESPONDING TO THE SCRIPTURES in Chapter 8.

8

Hospitality's Warm Embrace

Purpose

- To acknowledge the role of biblical hospitality in welcoming newcomers into the community of faith

Reading the Scriptures

Read and consider Genesis 18:1-15.
My first responses to this passage are ...

Exploring the Scriptures

In concluding our study we turn to the Old Testament and Genesis 18:1-15. These verses record the fascinating visit of three divine strangers to the household of Abraham and Sarah. Through this account we discover yet another con-

cept vital to the task of inviting and welcoming others–
showing hospitality.

The story of Abraham is told in Genesis 12–25. The story
begins with God's call to Abraham to leave his home and
move to a new land (Gen. 12). It continues with the story of
Abraham's separation from Lot (Gen. 13) and God's cove-
nant promises to Abraham and Sarah which include the
hope of a newborn son (Gen. 15-17). As we enter the events
of Genesis 18, Abraham and Sarah have settled in Mamre.
Mamre is a hilly settlement known for its great lush oak
forest. It is located south of Bethlehem, some two miles
north of Hebron.

The scriptures tell us that the Lord appears to Abraham
at Mamre (18:1) in the form of a stranger accompanied by
two companions. Seeing the three men, Abraham runs
from his tent door to meet them (v. 2). Quickly he takes
steps to provide them a royal welcome even though at this
point he is not aware of their divine identity (vv. 2-5). He
provides them water to wash their tired, dusty feet; he of-
fers them rest under the great oak trees and fetches them
"a morsel of bread." Actually the morsel turns out to be
quite a feast. Three measures of the very best meal, about
four pecks, is kneaded and made into a generous supply of
cakes. A fat, tender calf is slaughtered and prepared. Curds
and milk are brought out in abundant supply (vv. 6-8).

Why does Abraham go to such great lengths to offer hospitality to these strangers? Genesis commentator John
Gibson explains that Abraham's act of hospitality is not all
that surprising, but rather typical of the time.

> In the east, hospitality has always meant
> much more than holding a supper party or giv-
> ing a bed to a friend for the night–our usual
> understanding of the term. It means literally
> taking strangers into one's home, and is a
> highly esteemed virtue, particularly in a no-
> madic society such as Abraham's. In the eyes of
> such a society the guest is almost sacred, and

> any passing traveler, even a member of a hos-
> tile tribe, is entitled to become one.[1]

Later Hebrew writings in the book of Leviticus confirm
this description:

> When an alien resides with you in your land,
> you shall not oppress the alien. The alien who
> resides with you shall be to you as the citizen
> among you; you shall love the alien as yourself.
> (Lev. 19:33-34).

What is surprising is the intensity and extent of Abraham's hospitality. He goes way above and beyond the call
of duty in spite of not knowing the identity of his guests.

Once the meal is over, the visitors reveal the purpose of
their visit (18:9-10): to reaffirm the promise made by God (in
17:16-19) that a son would be born to Abraham and Sarah.
Sarah, standing behind Abraham at the door of the tent,
apparently out of sight, laughs softly to herself. She is 89,
hardly a prime candidate for childbearing! (18:11).

God responds to Sarah's laughter with a rhetorical question: "Is anything too hard for the Lord?" (18:14 NIV). The
answer, of course, is no, as affirmed throughout the history
of God's people. Jeremiah echoes this sentiment when he
declares to God, "Nothing is too difficult for you" (Jer. 32:17
TEV). The angel declares it to Mary saying, "For there is
nothing that God cannot do" (Luke 1:37 TEV). Jesus under-
scores this truth through his affirmation, "Everything is
possible for God" (Mark 10:27 TEV).

These words become flesh and blood reality a short time
later.

> The Lord visited Sarah as he had said, and the
> Lord did to Sarah as he had promised. And
> Sarah conceived, and bore Abraham a son ...
> Abraham called ... his son ... Isaac (Gen. 21:1-3
> TEV).

Appropriately, the promised child is named Isaac. The
word Isaac in Hebrew sounds like "he laughs" or "he

laughed." The story of Abraham, Sarah, and Isaac is a re-
minder to all generations that "God works with and
through people who laugh the laugh of doubt."[2]

Reflecting on the Scriptures

1. Who were the "three men"? You may have to go beyond
    this passage to answer this question.

2. Compare the importance of Abraham's action (hospital-
    ity) with God's action (the announcement of the child) in
    bringing about God's promises.

3. How important are the doubts of Sarah in blocking God's
    plan?

4. What other scriptures (if any) does this passage bring to
    mind?

Applying the Scriptures

Lovers of Strangers

Literally, the biblical word for hospitality, philoxenos, means "lover of strangers."[3] Such a root meaning should not surprise us. It comes directly out of the tradition of Abraham and the Israelite people.[4] As we have discovered through our scripture study, for Abraham and his descendants, "The alien. . . shall be to you as the citizen among you, and you shall love the alien as yourself" (Lev. 19:34).

Ironically, most of us have been encouraged to be leery of strangers. As Kenneth Gibble notes:

> In our world the assumption is that strangers are potentially dangerous.... When we travel, we keep a careful eye on our luggage; when we walk the streets, we are keenly aware of where we keep our money. We guard our homes with watchdogs and double locks, our roads with anti-hitchhike signs, ... our cities with armed police, and our country with missiles poised to launch atomic annihilation.[5]

The challenge is to move away from such suspicion and animosity. We need, in the words of Henri Nouwen, to move from hostility to hospitality. We do this, Nouwen says, as we begin to create free or open space in our individual lives and congregations where the stranger can enter and become a friend instead of an enemy. We live such busy lives. We are so preoccupied with our needs and our agenda. However, we will never discover the folks around us–let alone the stranger–unless we go out of our way to find time and space for other people.

As we make room for others, we make room for them to be themselves. Offering hospitality is not a ploy to assemble a captive audience for our stories, agenda, and interests. Rather, it is an opportunity we provide for the others, the strangers, to find their story. Henri Nouwen echoes this when he says:

> The paradox of hospitality is that it wants to create emptiness, not a fearful emptiness, but a friendly emptiness where strangers can enter and discover themselves as created free; free to sing their own songs, speak their own languages, dance their own dances, free also to leave and follow their own vocations. Hospitality is not a subtle invitation to adopt the life-style of the host, but the gift of a chance for the guest to find his own.[6]

My wife Cathy has a special gift for creating this kind of space, for providing meaningful hospitality. In the fall of 1987, she led the women of our church family in a prayer retreat at a nearby state park. The overnight retreat was a life-changing experience for a number of women, but especially for one of our newer members.

As I heard various accounts of the retreat it became obvious that Cathy's gift of hospitality created the climate for spiritual renewal to take place. Through her attention to detail, her ability to make persons feel welcome, and her caring, positive spirit, space was created for participants really to relax. Busy homemakers, who normally could not resist the urge to handle one more housekeeping detail, were able to let go and truly seek the Lord.

Welcome Home Friendliness

A prime opportunity for extending hospitality is the Sunday morning experience in the local church. Along with creating space in our individual lives for the stranger, we also need to create space in our congregations. Persons are attracted to communities of faith that exhibit a spirit of hospitality and "welcome home friendliness." Warren J. Hartman, research director of the United Methodist Church, says:

> When both unchurched and churched people
> are asked what they look for in a church...all
> of them agree about one factor–the climate of
> the congregation. They are looking for a
> church in which they feel at home, where the
> people are friendly, and where there is a warm
> and comfortable atmosphere.[7]

Changes in our society have made the need for friendly,
hospitable congregations especially urgent. At one time
"welcome home friendliness" was a regular part of what
we knew as small-town America. However, in today's fast-
paced, urbanized culture, we use people instead of relating
to them. The result: feelings of loneliness, alienation, and
lack of connectedness.[8]

How are you helping your congregation respond to this
urgent need? Are you aware of the strangers in your
midst? Do you personally go out of your way to greet and
welcome visitors? Do you care for newcomers, perhaps
through a meal, a card, or a visit?

The story is told of a pastor who visited a Coptic monas-
tery. It was in the middle of the desert, about a day's
journey from Cairo, Egypt. The monks treated him like roy-
alty. They served him a wonderful meal, showed him to
the best of rooms, and brought him a bouquet of flowers.
He was then personally greeted by the abbot of the monas-
tery, Father Jeremiah.

"Wow!" said the pastor. "You sure know how to treat
visitors."

Father Jeremiah replied, "We always treat guests as if
they were angels, just to be safe."[9]

The story of Abraham, Sarah, and the strangers certainly
confirms the wisdom of such an outlook. So do the words
of Jesus:

> Come, O blessed...inherit the kingdom pre-
> pared for you...for I was hungry and you gave
> me food, I was thirsty and you gave me drink, I
> was a stranger and you welcomed me...Then

the righteous will answer... "Lord... when did
we see thee a stranger and welcome thee?...
Truly I say to you, as you did it to one of the
least of these my brethren, you did it to me"
(Matt. 25:34-40).

Responding to the Scriptures

1. What are some of your best instances of receiving hospitality?

2. Who are some of the persons you know who have the gift of hospitality?

3. What are the marks of that gift?

4. How do you "create empty space" for others in which they might "find [their] own"?

5. What do you need to be a lover of strangers?

6. How do you act when you see a visitor to your congregation at a Sunday morning worship service?

7. How could you, and/or your congregation, be more hospitable to new persons on a Sunday morning?

8. What Good News of Jesus Christ can you convey to them through hospitality?

9. (To be completed following discussion) My learnings from this session are ...

10. Complete RESPONDING TO THE CALL FOR ACTION (found on the following page) and share your responses.

Responding to the Call for Action

1. The things I have learned which are calling me to invite and welcome are...

2. The persons I feel called to invite and welcome are...

3. In the next four weeks I will invite and welcome...

4. My invitations will include a message of...

I _____ will
ask _____ to help
me be accountable for the above actions.

Endnotes

Chapter 1. Witnesses, With Power!

1. Lloyd J. Ogilvie, Acts, in The Communicator's Commentary Series, vol. 5 (Waco, Texas: Word Books, 1983), p. 23.
2. William F. Arndt and F. Wilbur Gingrich, A Greek-English Lexicon of the New Testament (Chicago: University of Chicago Press, 1957), p. 206.
3. Gerhard Kittle and Gerhard Friedrich, eds., and Geoffrey W. Bromiley, trans., Theological Dictionary of the New Testament, in one volume abridged by Geoffrey W. Bromiley (Grand Rapids: William B. Eerdmans Publishing Company, 1985), pp. 564-565.
4. D. A. Carson, Exegetical Fallacies (Grand Rapids: Baker Book House, 1984), p. 35.
5. Anita and Peter Deyneka, "A Spiritual Odyssey," Christianity Today, vol. 32, no. 13 (September 16, 1988), pp. 17-23.
6. Halford E. Luccock, The Acts of the Apostles in Present Day Preaching (New York: Harper and Brothers Publishers, 1938), pp. 14-15.
7. Christine Michael, "Remembering Bill Bosler," New Beginnings (March, 1987).

Chapter 2. Beginning Where We Are

1. M. Burrows, "Jerusalem," in The Interpreter's Dictionary of the Bible, vol. 2 (Nashville: Abingdon Press, 1962), pp. 843-844.

2. R. Laird Harris, Gleason L. Archer, Jr., Bruce K. Waitke, eds., Theological Wordbook of the Old Testament, vol. 2 (Chicago: Moody Press, 1980), p. 942.
3. Lawrence O. Richards, A Theology of Christian Education (Grand Rapids: Zondervan Publishing House, 1975), p. 36.
4. "Don't Stop Inviting," NetResults vol. 6, no. 46 (January, 1985), p. 2.
5. C. Wayne Zunkel, Church Growth Under Fire (Scottdale, Pennsylvania: Herald Press, 1987), p. 132.
6. "Don't Stop Inviting," p. 2.
7. Merlin E. Garber, "Accept the Mandate, Receive the Power, and Go," in Call the Witnesses, ed. Paul M. Robinson (Elgin, Illinois: The Brethren Press, 1974), p. 77.
8. J. Wascom Pickett, Christian Mass Movements in India (1933), pp. 43-45, cited in George G. Hunter III, To Spread the Power (Nashville: Abingdon Press, 1987), pp. 92-93.
9. George G. Hunter III, The Contagious Congregation (Nashville: Abingdon Press, 1979), p. 34.

Chapter 3. In Samaria?

1. William Barclay, The Gospel of John, vol. 1 (Philadelphia: The Westminster Press, 1975), p. 147.
2. Sam Keen, commentator, PBS documentary "Faces of the Enemy" (Berkeley, California: A Quest Production for the Catticus Corporation, 1987).
3. James S. Hewett, ed., Illustrations Unlimited (Wheaton, Illinois: Tyndale House Publishers, Inc., 1988), p. 214.
4. Roger L. Fredrikson, John, in The Communicator's Commentary Series, vol. 4 (Waco, Texas: Word Books, 1985), p. 94.
5. Rebecca Manley Pippert, Out of the Saltshaker and into the World (Downers Grove, Illinois: InterVarsity Press, 1979), pp. 177-178.

Chapter 4. To the Ends of the Earth

1. Donald A. McGavran, Understanding Church Growth (Grand
   Rapids: William B. Eerdmans Publishing Company, 1980),
   p. 56.
2. William Barclay, The Gospel of Luke (Philadelphia: The
   Westminster Press, 1975), p. 199.
3. James I. Packer, Merrill C. Tenny, and William White, Jr.,
   eds., The Bible Almanac (Nashville: Thomas Nelson
   Publishers, 1980), p. 333.
4. Barclay, p. 203.
5. Leslie R. Keylock, "Spokesman for the Cities," Moody
   Monthly, vol. 89, no. 3 (November, 1988), pp. 70-72.

Chapter 5. The Receptive Moment

1. Merrill F. Unger, Unger's Bible Dictionary (Chicago:
   Moody Press, 1959), p. 328.
2. Yohanan Aharoni and Michael Avi-Yonah, The
   Macmillan Bible Atlas (New York: Macmillan
   Publishing Company, Inc., 1968), p. 152.
3. Arndt and Gingrich, p. 507.
4. William Barclay, The Acts of the Apostles (Philadelphia:
   The Westminster Press, 1976), pp. 68-69.
5. Lloyd J. Ogilvie, Drumbeat of Love (Waco, Texas: Word
   Books, 1976), p. 116.
6. Archibald Thomas Robertson, Word Pictures in the New
   Testament, vol. 3 (Nashville: Broadman Press, 1930), p. 110.
7. William Nell, The Acts of the Apostles (Greenwood,
   South Carolina: The Attic Press, Inc., 1973), p. 125.
8. Joe Harding quoted in "How to Accelerate 'Invitation
   Evangelism,'" Net Results, vol. 6, no. 46 (January, 1985), p.
   1.
9. Ogilvie, Drumbeat of Love, pp. 119-120.
10. Ibid., p. 122.
11. McGavran, p. 248.

Chapter 6. An Invitation That Fits

1. K. W. Clark, "Sea of Galilee," in The Interpreter's Dictionary of the Bible, vol. 2 (Nashville: Abingdon Press, 1962), pp. 348-350.
2. William Barclay, The Gospel of Matthew, vol. 1 (Philadelphia: The Westminster Press, 1975), p. 77.
3. Kittle, Friedrich, and Bromiley, p. 556.
4. Myron S. Augsburger, Matthew in The Communicators Commentary Series, vol. 1 (Waco, Texas: Word Books, 1982) p. 55.
5. Robertson, p. 35.
6. George A. Buttrick, "The Gospel According to St. Matthew: Exposition," in The Interpreter's Bible, vol. 7 (Nashville: Abingdon Press, 1951), p. 276.
7. David Augsburger, Witness is Withness (Chicago: Moody Press, 1971), p. 118.
8. Yancey, Philip, "Helping Those in Pain," Leadership, Volume 5, Number 2 (Spring 1984), p. 97.
9. Arthur G. McPhee, "Friendship Evangelism in the Third Way," in Witnesses of a Third Way, ed. Henry J. Schmidt (Elgin, Illinois: Brethren Press, 1986), p. 86.
10. Pippert, p. 130.

Chapter 7. Sharing, But Also Caring

1. William Barclay, The Gospel of Luke (Philadelphia: The Westminster Press, 1975), p. 234.
2. David A. Anderson, All the Trees and Woody Plants of the Bible (Waco, Texas: Word Books, 1979), pp. 143-144, 222.
3. Bruce Larson, Luke, in The Communicator's Commentary Series, vol. 3 (Waco, Texas: Word Books, 1983), p. 271.
4. Barclay, Luke, p. 235.
5. Ibid.
6. David Augsburger, pp. 52-53.

7. Armstrong, Richard, The Pastor as Evangelist, (Philadelphia: The Westminster Press, 1984), pp. 37-38.
8. Win Arn and Charles Arn, "Six Steps to Effective Disciple Making," in The Pastors Church Growth Handbook, vol. 2, ed. Win Arn (Pasadena, California: Church Growth Press, 1982), pp. 98-99.

Chapter 8. Hospitality's Warm Embrace

1. John C. L. Gibson, Genesis, vol. 2 (Philadelphia: The Westminster Press, 1982), pp. 75-76.
2. Eugene F. Roop, Genesis, in Believers Church Bible Commentary (Scottdale, Pennsylvania: Herald Press, 1987), p. 127.
3. Bruce A. Rowlison, Creative Hospitality (Alhambra, California: Green Leaf Press, 1981), p. 30.
4. Gerhard Kittel and Gerhard Friedrich, eds., and Geoffrey W. Bromley, trans., Theological Dictionary of the New Testament, vol. 5 (Grand Rapids: William B. Eerdmans Publishing Company, 1967), pp. 8-20.
5. Kenneth L. Gibble, "Hospitality to Strangers," Brethren Life and Thought, vol. 26, no. 3 (Summer, 1981), p. 185.
6. Henri J. M. Nouwen, Reaching Out (Garden City, New York: Doubleday and Company, 1975), p. 51.
7. Herb Miller, How to Build a Magnetic Church (Nashville: Abingdon Press, 1987), p. 64.
8. Ibid.
9. Ibid., p. 63.